Grind Don't Quit

Jamie Holtom
and
Jim Christian

 FriesenPress

One Printers Way
Altona, MB R0G 0B0
Canada

www.friesenpress.com

Copyright © 2024 by Jamie Holtom and Jim Christian
First Edition — 2024

ISBN
978-1-03-919403-8 (Hardcover)
978-1-03-919402-1 (Paperback)
978-1-03-919404-5 (eBook)

Self-Help, Motivational & Inspirational

Distributed to the trade by The Ingram Book Company

Introducing Ourselves

My name is Jamie Holtom, and I've been in ministry at North Bramalea United Church in Brampton, Ontario for almost twenty-five years. I'm married to Katrina, a high school math teacher at a local school in our community. We have three kids who are quite different from one another and all amazing in their own way.

In both my life and leadership, I've experienced the realities of this book. The need to "grind and not quit" has been instrumental to everything I've done. There are always moments along the way when you wonder if you're going to make it, if it's worth it, or if you can do it, and sometimes you just need that little bit of encouragement that says "Keep going! You can do it!"

Our hope is that you'll find that kind of encouragement from reading this book. Especially through the last few years and the pandemic, the need for encouragement has never been greater. Many times, I've felt like giving up because it's been so hard, so complex, so uncertain, so challenging!

This book will cover several topics that I think you'll find interesting and helpful, but also hopeful. It's good to know that you're not the only one who struggles. It's good to feel like others experience what you experience. It's good to find people who have worked through some of the same kinds of challenges in life and in leadership.

You can read the book through from cover to cover or find a topic you like and dive into it one chapter at a time. Each chapter contains an introduction to a concept, a story to help highlight and keep it real, some practical ideas on how to apply the content, a personal story from friends whose story aligns with that chapter's concept, and a prayer of encouragement to help you "grind, don't quit."

You may be wondering where the title of this book came from? That's a great question! My good friend Jim Christian coined this phrase at tough time in his life, and he's been living into it as well as anyone I know!

***

My name is Jim Christian, founder and CEO of Cornerstone Building and Property Services Inc. Cornerstone is a construction and project management firm that services clients across North America, with approximately thirty people on the team. I've been married to Sherry for over forty years, and together we attend North Bramalea United Church and are active in various ministries there that Jamie leads.

In addition to serving and leading at Cornerstone, I'm also active in the community. I like to say I have a PHD from the University of Hard Knocks, and a few years ago I was getting knocked around. Luckily for me, Jamie and I started a journey of personal development together to grow in our lives and leadership, so when these knocks came, Jamie was on the journey with me! We decided to author this book in hopes that it might inspire readers to keep grinding when they're ready to quit. We both acknowledge that an inner strength to "grind, don't quit" comes from a relationship with Jesus, empowered by the Holy Spirit, but we also know that we have a part to play.

CHAPTER ONE:

When You Feel Like Giving Up

INTRODUCTION

Have you ever felt like giving up?

Maybe you'd reached the end of your rope. Perhaps the challenges to finish the project were just too much. Maybe you found yourself at a point where you couldn't see hope no matter how positive and resilient you usually are.

Everyone has been there! You are not alone! I know I've felt that way, and my good friend Jim sure was in that place on our flight from Nashville back to Brampton in the fall of 2018. Jim was in one of the most challenging years of his life. Business had deteriorated, and he had lost some of his best staff, as they decided to move on for several reasons.

During all of this, he'd been working harder than ever but with no results and what seemed like only bad news on the horizon. I had never seen Jim so deflated and down. As he expressed his concerns and poured out his heart, there didn't seem to be anything I could say to help him. He was lost in the paralysis of analysis, and it was a deep, dark hole that was getting bigger and bigger. It was the longest ninety-minute flight I've ever had!

And then just as we arrived in Toronto, we somehow landed together on this idea that seemed to resonate for Jim and brought back some life, energy, and hope! It was simply this: GRIND, DON'T QUIT!

***

On reflection, I didn't realize that it was the longest ninety-minute flight Jamie had ever had, but it was a dark discussion for sure. It resulted in me taking small actions that I could control, because at the time it didn't feel like I had much control at all. I just had to grind and not quit doing things that I could control. Business was falling apart around me, and there wasn't much I could control. But I could control how I started my day to set myself up to be the healthiest I could be. So I started a morning ritual of devotions, reading, journaling, and exercising every day, rain or shine, if I felt like it or not. Looking back, it seems strange that with a huge business challenge, I focused on myself, but it gave me the energy to fight and to grind, not quit. I think it built my confidence that I could do hard things.

That spilled into my daily activities in the company when I had to do the hard things, things I could control. "Grind, don't quit" would become a mantra for the next year or so. It would be my guiding principle each day. And in the end, it paid off!

Grind, don't quit!

Getting Real

The story of Terry Fox shows the mindset and the heart behind "grind, don't quit." Terry set out to run across Canada to raise money and awareness around cancer research. That's an unbelievable feat! And the way he did it makes it even more incredible. Terry decided he was going to run a marathon a day. That's approximately forty-three kilometres a day! Making this feat even more significant, he was well into his battle with cancer and had had one of his legs amputated, so he was doing all of this on one leg!

The image of Terry hobbling as he ran with that little hop step is unforgettable. Talk about grinding it out through what must have seemed impossible! There were many days when it was raining and cold, and there was Terry putting in his time and his miles each day!

I once heard Terry's brother Fred Fox share how Terry did it when he was speaking at a school assembly. Terry kept saying to himself as he ran, "Just make it to the next light pole." And then the next. And the next. And the next. One light pole at a time was all Terry did. He wasn't thinking about the whole trek across the country. He wasn't even thinking about the entire forty-three kilometres for that day. Just one light pole at a time!

Whatever you're facing as you begin to read this book, our hope and prayer is that God enables you to keep going. Like Terry Fox, no matter what challenges you face, simply get to that next light pole and then see what happens from there. Terry faced lots of challenges, but all these years later his impact continues to be felt because he certainly knew what it meant to "grind, don't quit!"

Sometimes we want to give up because it just feels too hard. Jim was certainly in that place, and I know I've been there many times as well. Although I wouldn't consider myself a runner, I have been running for years off and on as a way of getting some exercise and staying healthy. It amazes me how hard the first couple of kilometres can be—every time! It just takes some time for my body to warm up. I find it hard to breathe at first until I get into a bit of a flow. Many times, I want to stop and walk or just turn around and go home. But after getting through that first little bit, I find a rhythm where I start to feel good. I not only catch my breath but find a good pace, where breathing becomes natural, and I start to relax. It almost becomes easy. (Yes, almost!)

You may find that too. And not just in running. This also applies to life and leadership.

Maybe it's hard to get going. You might feel paralyzed and unsure of where to start. Or you know exactly what you need to do but you're afraid or don't know if you have it in you. We hope this book helps with these things. But here's the point for now:

> *If you keep going, it will get easier—maybe not easy, but easier!*

Sometimes you just need to grind it out!

WAYS TO LIVE THIS OUT

What does all this mean for us as we try to live into it? What can those who want to give up do to take some steps toward a better future, whatever that might be?

1. Acknowledge the pain: Don't be afraid to name your current reality. We can acknowledge where we're at and that we want to give up, or that we're wondering if we have it in us. Sometimes the first step to healing,

recovery, or a new path forward is to own where we are and how hard it is, and to know that's ok!

2. Ask for help: Reach out. Let someone know how you're feeling. You can use this as an opportunity to be real with someone about where you're at. It could be a counsellor, friend, partner, or colleague.

3. Do something, even if it's a small thing: We don't have to do it all at once. We don't have to do everything today. Just do something, even on thing, that will move the needle a little. There's a chapter coming up about just taking one step, and it's so important. We may not see the complete picture, or even believe it can happen, but just do one thing today and go from there. These small steps will build your confidence to keep moving forward one step at a time.

4. Be open: We encourage you to read this book to move past that real and understandable feeling of wanting to give up. At this point, just be open. We hope you will find a way forward through some of the thoughts and ideas presented here. In fact, that's one of our greatest prayers. You are part of the reason we put this down, and if it helps even one person, it will have been worth it!

As we begin this journey together, hopefully it's apparent that we all have seasons and days when we feel like giving up. It's a part of life and being human. It doesn't just happen to some people. It's not just you. It happens to every single one of us. Leaders who don't feel ready for the challenges of the day. Single parents simply trying to make ends meet. People grieving the loss of a loved one, unsure if they can carry on. People or loved ones experiencing health challenges. Young people doubting themselves and wondering if anyone cares about them. Middle aged folks challenged to see a bigger future than their current reality. Broken relationships with family or life-long friends.

We have a choice to make—to keep going despite the challenges, barriers, to not give up and lose hope. It's not an easy decision, but it's possible. There are people just like you who make that decision every day. You can make it today, right now, in this very moment. And as you do, please know that you're not alone. There are people cheering for you. People who have gone before you.

People who are thinking about you right now. People who may know you better than you know yourself.

We are cheering for you! That's why we wrote this book, because we've been there too and will be again, and we know that we all need someone to cheer us on. We encourage you to keep going, and even when you don't feel like going on, know that you have another gear. You can choose life and a future. You choose to grind it out and not give up.

As you'll see in the next chapter, it may just be the best decision you'll ever make!

A PERSONAL STORY—DR. JUSTINE BLAINEY-BROKER

I am that girl who wanted to play hockey with the boys! I wanted what my brother was able to have and I wasn't because I was a girl. I fought through the courts and won at the Supreme Court of Canada for equality in sports to be able to play on the boys' hockey team.

I was hated. I was told by family that I was disgracing the family name. I was bullied and disowned by friends. I was harassed on buses and subway cars. Teachers slammed doors in my face and tried to fail me in school. I would do anything to hang out with anyone, including hanging out in groups engaged in underage drinking and with bad crowds that eventually hurt me.

Even though I grew up in a Catholic family, I thought that if there was a God, the world could *not* be this evil, unjust, and mean. I felt that I never fit in anywhere as a young feminist. My mantra was "If it's to be, it's up to me." I learned to work harder than anyone else I knew. I constantly wanted to quit the fight, but my mother would say, "Just sleep on it and decide in the morning." Somehow in the morning things seemed brighter and I had more hope.

I was a "wanna-be" with respect to believing in God and fitting in at church. I truly felt very alone, on the outside looking in. Thankfully I met my amazing husband, who had so much faith in God and in me that he chose to stick by me, knowing that at some point I'd find my way. We searched through numerous churches to find some place where I'd feel comfortable in my disbelief. My children chose North Bramalea United Church, and I felt welcomed because they said that I could belong even before I believed.

With great thanks to my husband, Blake, Jamie, and my chiropractic family, I was rebaptized approximately fifteen years ago. I still struggle at times when bad things happen, but I'm more open now to the miracles of God too!

My new mantra is "if it's to be. It's up to God and me!"

A PRAYER OF ENCOURAGEMENT

Dear God,
Sometimes I feel like giving up because it's so hard to keep going.
There are moments along the way when I just don't feel like I have it in me.
I pray for strength to continue, especially when it's hard.
Help me to put one foot in front of the other
And trust that one day it will get easier.
Amen!

CHAPTER TWO:

The Biggest Decision!

INTRODUCTION

Do you have things on your to do list that you know you should do? You know that once you do them, you'll move toward your goal, but you just don't feel like it? The resistance is too great, or maybe you see an objection coming. You can't find it in yourself to act. The mountain just seems too high to climb, or you don't think you have what it takes—the skill, the knowledge, or both. This is the time when you must find a way to dig deep and take action, because if you wait for the right mood or the perfect conditions, it may never happen. Our experience has been that mood follows action!

We'll share many examples of this throughout the book, but for me, committing to getting healthy was that mountain. I had to accept that I was worthy of selfcare and acknowledge that people were counting on me to be healthy and lead. I had to accept that I was obese and that I had never felt athletic or been athletic, nor was I ever encouraged to be. In my mind, I didn't have any natural abilities, and it just seemed an impossible mountain to climb. I was probably over 280 pounds (I quit weighing myself at 275), had been on high blood pressure pills for decades, couldn't walk the golf course, and just kept getting bigger and bigger clothes to hide in. I felt terrible, and I didn't like the way I looked, especially in pictures. My low self-esteem just got lower and lower, and my health continued to deteriorate. The only two things going up were my weight and the amount I ate and drank!

But that all changed once I got a picture in my eye of what it could be like, a vision for my life and health. That vision collided with my dissatisfaction with my reality. It took a year, but it was a series of explosions ending with one big explosion when during a sleepless night in a hotel in San Diego at 2:00 AM, I realized that I was fast-tracking to a heart attack, stroke, diabetes, and alcoholism, and it had to stop.

Getting control of my health was step one in this journey, because I couldn't achieve my vision for my life without being healthy and energetic. But there was a big problem—exercise was not something that came naturally to me.

GETTING REAL

I was waiting for the day that it would come naturally and that I'd love it so much that I'd miss it if it didn't happen. I wanted to get healthy, wanted the runners high, but I needed to act. It took months, but now I get it, and now I miss it if I don't exercise and get that high.

My health journey had many twists and turns, successes, and setbacks, but I can't tell you the number of times I would repeat to myself, "Mood follows action, mood follows action," and then I would do my routine. In the early days, it was a thirty-minute walk, and then I started to do push-ups. I was embarrassed how few I could do, but gradually every day I took a little quicker walk and did a few more push-ups. Every day grinding, not quitting. Then I started doing body weight exercises, a thing called Tabata, and I started to walk faster. Then I added short sprints of running, gradually getting to the point where I was running as much as I was walking, then running more than I was walking. Grinding, not quitting, every day. Then I started doing strength training.

Yes, there are still hard days, and I don't want to do it, but that's when I go back to mood follows action, and before I know it, my routine is over and I'm feeling energized.

Jamie:

I just want to add a couple thoughts here. I remember Jim in those early days and how he was challenged to continue, especially on those days when his body was sore and tired. He would text me, asking when it was going to get easier. But then he would do it! He'd keep walking, and then before long, he was running. He'd keep doing strength training, even when he could barely walk, he was so sore. He did NOT feel like exercising. But he did it anyway!

Then one day I remember he told me that he couldn't imagine NOT exercising every morning. In fact, he said his body craved exercise. It was awesome! I realized how far he'd come!

All those mornings exercising when he didn't feel like it had paid off in a big way! He also grew in his ability to participate in all kinds of sports, and though he occasionally slips into the mental mindset of his early years, that "he's not an athlete," those moments are rare these days. He's a new guy, a different person, an athlete who loves to be active! But it all started with that decision all those years ago!

You may be asking how you can do it, as your mountain seems bigger than mine, or you think you don't have what it takes. But let us assure you—you do have what it takes. You can do it. We believe in you.

WAYS TO LIVE THIS OUT

Here are some practical ideas for you to start climbing the mountain.

1. Capture a Vision of Your Future Self

We aren't sure how you see your future self, but you do. You may see people doing what you want to be doing—owning a business, being dedicated to a ministry, involved in a type of relationship you desire, being fit and healthy, walking close to God. Start to examine their lives and habits. Explore how they achieved these things and start to get a sense of how you want your ideal life to be.

Seek clarity, meet with people, ask them questions about their lives, what books they're reading, podcasts they're listening to, and start doing the same. At the same time, start writing a vision for your life or an area of your life so that you get a clear grasp of what could be.

The most important thing is to be clear and concise about what you want to become in three years, ten years, and twenty-five years. This will become fuel in the explosion you want to create when it collides with your current reality.

2. Feel the Pain

Live in the pain of your present reality, get emotional, cry, yell, get frustrated, and hold it in your mind. Let the disappointment rise in you. This may be one big event, or it may be a long, slow burn, or both. Our experience has been that if you don't sit in it, you won't get the motivation, the drive, the energy to push through the resistance that will come.

We'd encourage you to change how you look at these emotions, seeing them not as negative but as positive, because this will be the well you tap into gain energy and momentum for the transformation you're looking for. Write all these reasons down, preferably in a journal using pen and paper, because research has shown that the mind engages differently when writing rather than typing. This writing will create your own explosion so that you can create a future vision for this area of your life. You can change. You have more agency over yourself than you think.

3. Get Clear on Your Why

You now have a picture of what you want to become, and you're now totally dissatisfied with your current reality. Now you must get clear on why you want to accomplish the goal! This will fuel you when the going gets tough. Gail Hyatt says, "People who lose their why lose their way," and that is so true.

Your why must be personal, inspire you, and give you hope.

For me, it was a combination of several factors, but the main thrust was that I had too many people counting on me to be healthy and the best me I could be.

Develop a personal statement about what you want to accomplish, write it in the present tense, and read it every day. Hang it on a wall or a mirror—anywhere you might look when you don't want to act. Find pictures to represent the statement, or slogans that you can write, print, look at, or read. Surround yourself with things that represent your why so that when your commitment wains, you have solid reminders.

This is digging a little deeper into why you want to achieve your vision. It's demanding work, but you just keep asking, "Why?" We'd encourage you to work at discovering your why and get as clear as possible.

Because the going will get tough and you'll face resistance and obstacles, you will have to pivot, adapt, and be creative. Your why is what you'll hold on to. As the old saying goes, "When the going gets tough, the tough get going." We would add, "Only if they know their why."

In our experience, this why must be greater than yourself. You're answering a higher calling from God, the creator. You've been put on this world for a purpose, and that's your why. It's been said that the two most important days of a person's life are the day they were born and the day they discover why.

4. Keep Score!

Find a way to track your progress, and break it down to daily action. This goes for any goal. Reports say that when he was starting out, Jerry Seinfeld had a goal to write one joke a day. As he did it, he'd put a big X on a wall calendar. This showed his progress and gamified the process, because then it became a game to not break the chain.

Here are a few ideas on how to break a goal down to daily action:

You want to lose weight and get healthier. Start tracking your daily exercise and commitment to thirty minutes a day, even if it's just a walk. Mark it as "achieved" when you do it. Focus on not breaking the chain.

You want to learn to play the piano. Decide to practise fifteen minutes a day and track it. Focus on not breaking the chain.

You want to have a better relationship with someone, perhaps a spouse, child, or friend. Choose an activity you can do every day to improve that relationship. It may be a quick call, a text message, a true face to face chat, a facetime call, writing a note and putting it in the mail, sending flowers, grabbing a coffee together, or doing something together that the other person usually does by themselves. Decide, track it, and focus on not breaking the chain.

Maybe you want to deepen your connection with God. Decide on what you can do daily to start building that connection, such as daily morning prayer, a short online devotional, an app to read the Bible in one year. You get the idea: decide, track, and focus on not breaking the chain.

The reality is the chain will be broken. When it breaks, have grace with yourself and realize that life can get in the way sometimes, then focus on when you want to start again. It can be the next day or two days from now or a week from now, but commit to starting again.

If you can't find the commitment in you to start again, look at your why, review your notes on the discomfort or pain that the present reality is causing, and review your notes on the goal and why it was important. You'll have a choice to make: you can recommit, revise, or change the goal, and change the vision for something that's better for you. It's your goal, it's your vision, so you have agency over it.

There will be many twists, turns, and difficulties along the way, but you can hold on to the vision tightly and the strategy loosely. There's more than one way to get to where you're going. Just like when you're planning a driving trip, you plan your route, but you may come upon construction, traffic jams, detours, and roadblocks. You don't give up on the trip—you make a course correction and keep moving in the direction you set out to go. Capturing your vision is no different.

I want to share a little more about my journey in the first six months of deciding to get healthy and lose weight. I started with walking every day and counting calories to reset my portion control. I had committed to everyday exercise every morning as part of my morning ritual. So I made tick marks when I exercised every day, and tick marks for days I ate under 2,400 calories.

After starting, Jamie encouraged me to add some additional exercise and to do push-ups after my walk. He said there was a challenge of doing five hundred push-ups at one time, and that should be my goal. That was clearly in my delusional zone, as I hadn't done push-ups for several years. I thought, *Well, let's start doing some push-ups every day.* The idea was to do as many push-ups in a minute as I could and then rest the balance of the minute. Then I'd start again and keep going until I couldn't go anymore.

Well, it was ugly. The first day I did two push-ups and no additional minutes, and day two was the same, day 3 on my knees getting worse. But even if I did one push up, I gave myself a tick mark. Eventually I was going three minutes with five to eight push-ups a minute, getting a tick mark each day. Then I moved to ten minutes, and in July, I did five hundred push-ups in twenty-six minutes! I achieved this goal one day at a time, one tick at a time. Grinding, not quitting!

A funny side story to this push up challenge, which I started in mid to late January. In March, Jamie and I travelled to Nashville for our quarterly coaching session with Michael Hyatt. Jamie was working hard at building my confidence in my ability to exercise. We were doing a morning routine and we finished, but I said I needed to do my push-ups for eight minutes, so Jamie joined me, and we did our push-ups. The next day we did the same thing, but when I said I had to do my push-ups at the end of the routine, he told me that I should only be doing them once a week. I looked shocked and said something to the effect of "When you told me about this challenge, you said daily." So the debate started about his instructions on the challenge! It was funny at the time for him, but that only increased my resolve to keep doing them daily. One tick at a time!

The biggest decision you'll ever make is that you can achieve a vision for your life, or any area of your life, if you grind and don't quit! Get clear on what you want to achieve, stir up emotions about what you don't like about the present, get clear on your why, and keep track of your actions. Things will change, and obstacles will come; however, you can learn from your failures and setbacks. You've found a way that doesn't work. You can hold on to your vision tightly, your strategies loosely, and have grace with yourself every step of the way.

The reality I faced with my health was a huge mountain. My doctor had given up on me and told me that I would be on high blood pressure pills for the rest of my life. When I asked what I could do, I could tell he didn't have much hope for me. He said "Move more and eat less!"

When I went back to him after losing over sixty pounds, he said, "What did you do?" I told him that I'd followed his advice; I'd moved more and eaten less. He said, "This is the biggest transformation I've seen in a long time." He still didn't hold much hope that I'd get off my blood pressure medication, which I'd been on for decades, but in December 2020, I was taken off the medication. It sure sounded simple to follow that advice, but it was hard.

We have both overcome significant obstacles in our lives by applying these principles. If we can do it as ordinary guys, living ordinary lives, then we have a desire to bless our families, friends, our organizations and contribute to the world.

If we can, you can too. You can overcome your challenges and obstacles and take advantage of opportunities. All you must do is grind, don't quit!

PERSONAL STORY—GARNETT MANNING

Ready or Not, Here I Come.
One negative but well-intentioned word of advice has the potential to derail your destiny.

It happened to me on the threshold of one of the most significant junctions in my life. Long before people of all racial and cultural backgrounds began to feel comfortable running for positions of leadership in Brampton, I took a chance, knowing the unlikeliness of being successful.

With no prior political experience or mentorship, I was driven with a passion that Brampton needed ethnic diversity at city hall and a stronger focus on the city's growing youth population. I spent four years learning about the city and the role of a city councillor. With this, the support of my family, and my faith in God, I felt confident that I was ready for the role.

Still, on one January day of 2003, prior to making my run for council official, I decided to make one more phone call to a man who had run in the previous election as the only Black candidate. He hadn't been successful, but I respected him as a role model and pioneer. Our conversation went something like this:

"Hey ____. How are you? This is Garnett Manning. I've decided to run for a seat on Brampton council, and I'd appreciate your support and a few tips."

There was a brief pause, then in a kind but cautionary tone he said, *"My friend, don't waste your time. Brampton is not ready for a Black city councillor."*

I was shocked and disappointed, as I wasn't expecting such an answer, but I quickly regained my composure, thanked him, and ended the call. For a moment, my mind believed that he could be right!

Then I had a hard conversation with myself. Success was possible! Why? In my fifteen years of living in Brampton, no one told me if they were ready for me.

That day I decided, *"Ready or not, here I come!"*

I ran, I won, and the rest is history.

Too often people have relinquished their plans, passion, and brilliance to fictitious elements. It's so important to know that readiness is a personal decision between the heart, mind, and God.

When you're ready, everything else will line up.

PRAYER OF ENCOURAGEMENT

God,
Thank you for the opportunity to grow and work through my current challenges.
You are a great provider, and I trust that you can give me all that I need to keep going,
especially when I don't feel like it.
When I'm tired, give me energy.
When I'm afraid, make me brave enough to try.
You have already given me all that I need to continue.
Thank you!
Amen.

CHAPTER THREE:

The Source of Resiliency

INTRODUCTION

It doesn't matter how strong, determined, and committed we are. We all reach a point where it's just too much on our own. Don't get me wrong—we're all about hard work, gritting your teeth, and keeping on keeping on. We're all about doing it even when you don't feel like it. You'll read about all these things in the chapters that follow. Yet there are moments and seasons when even that isn't enough. In our experience, we need a source of resiliency beyond our own means.

We just can't write this book and share our stories without pointing to this source of resiliency. At the end of the day, it's not *just* sheer determination and hard work. There's an opportunity here to lean into something greater than just our own willpower and effort. This is what we refer to in this chapter as "the source of resiliency." Some may call it a "Higher Power." Others may refer to this source as "Creator." We would name it the God who has come in Jesus and given us the Holy Spirit to energize, fuel, and empower us each day, especially when we've reached the end of our own ropes!

As you read this chapter, our hope is that we enter a "judgement-free zone." We're not suggesting that your beliefs need to be the same as ours. In no way are we claiming to have the whole "faith thing" figured out. We won't judge you or where you're at in this conversation, and we hope you'll do the same for us.

We invite you to enter this chapter as open as you can and see what might happen. It's an effective way not only to read a book like this but also to go about life.

GETTING REAL

My cousin James Hayward came to a point in his life where he realized that he just couldn't do it on his own. He was struggling with addiction in a way that was destroying him. At the age of thirty-two, he had a heart attack, and it was clear that he was in deep trouble if things didn't change.

The bigger issue was that James *knew* he needed to get healthy and stop drinking, and that if he didn't, he wouldn't see many more birthdays. However, it's one thing to *know* something but another to get it done! And making this life change wasn't one he could do on his own. Believe me, it wasn't for lack of effort. It wasn't that he hadn't tried. It wasn't that he didn't want to make this change. That is where he was forced to lean into this source of resiliency.

One night after an Alpha session (Alpha is a Christian basics course for people who are curious), James said a prayer that would change the trajectory of his life. He simply named to God that he wasn't able to beat this on his own. He had reached the end of his rope and wanted to be free from his addiction to alcohol, and the only way he was going to be able to do it was if God helped him make this change.

There was something about the surrendering of this over to God's resources. It wasn't that he wouldn't still be involved. James would need to play his part. In the days, weeks, and months and years ahead, James would have to do things like take care of himself, get counselling, connect to worship on a Sunday morning, make good choices over and over and over again. Talk about "grind, don't quit!"

However, something changed that night.

James had this overwhelming sense that he wasn't fighting this battle on his own. He had tapped into the greatest source of resiliency we have, if we're open to it. Again, we name it differently depending on our heritage, upbringing, culture, and where we grew up. There are many stories of people who surrendered to a higher power in ways just like this that allowed them to do things they could never have done on their own. It doesn't make it easy. However, it does make it more possible.

It's like plugging something into an electrical outlet. That appliance or equipment is still being used. It's still very much involved. However, a source of power enables it to work in a way that it couldn't on its own.

In this chapter, we'll describe how impactful this source of life and power and strength can be, and we'll invite you to consider how this might work in your own life. Absolutely no pressure, and if this "isn't your thing," feel free to move on to the next chapter or simply read with openness and curiosity.

Some of us may have drawn on this kind of power over the years but kind of lost our way and forgotten what a difference this kind of faith and relationship with God can make. This chapter might serve as a reminder and also a renewal of that kind of work in our lives and leadership.

Either way, we hope and pray that this source of resiliency helps you face your challenges and reminds you that you don't need to go it alone.

During times of challenge, we often find that people are more open to something beyond themselves. That's the power of leaning into a source of life, strength, and creativity beyond our own means. That's what we're suggesting here as the source of this resiliency we all seek and that can enable us to do far more than we can imagine.

I'm amazed at the resiliency of those who fight for justice. The anti-racism demonstrations that took place after the George Floyd tragedy of May 25, 2020, helped me to recognize in a new way the work that needed to be done to bring systemic change in light of the racism that is still so prevalent today. As I have worked with Black brothers and sisters and heard more of their stories and experiences, I've been blessed by the depth of faith in a God who will redeem and bring reconciliation and freedom. For many, there is a spiritual depth and a life of prayer and reliance on God that has brought a resiliency and commitment to keep working for justice.

What would it look like for us to bring this kind of faithfulness and expectation into our lives and leadership? As we open ourselves to this, or renew our commitment, several things may begin to happen. We will find a peace that enables us to not only survive the challenges we face but even to thrive amid them.

I saw a quote recently that said, "We can't change the waves, but we can learn to surf." Somehow as we lean into a source of resiliency, or a faith in a God who walks with us and leads us each day, we can find this inner peace and strength that starts to ground us. As we live and lead within this peace of God, we will be able to make better decisions and be a more positive influence on those around us. We will find a strength we didn't know we had.

There is a character in the Bible named Paul, often referred to as "the apostle Paul." The word apostle means "one who is sent." Paul had a clear purpose. He had been led to build the early church. However, he faced many barriers and challenges. One of the biggest challenges was that people who were spreading news about Jesus at the time were often persecuted for what they were doing. As a result, Paul ended up spending much of his time in prison. It would have been long days of darkness with little food in less-than-ideal circumstances. Despite these challenges, the apostle Paul never gave up. He continued to serve and lead. He wrote many letters from prison to the early churches, and he never complained. He had this tenacity and resilience that clearly came from something greater than himself.

In Philippians 4:6–7 Paul writes:

> Do not worry about anything, but in everything by prayer and supplication with thanksgiving let your requests be made known to God. And the peace of God, which surpasses all understanding, will guard your hearts and your minds in Christ Jesus.

As we lean into this source of resiliency, we also discover an energy and joy that we couldn't have on our own. Every morning I'm amazed at how my beautiful morning ritual enables me to enter the day differently. On many days, I wake up feeling a little overwhelmed at what lies ahead for me. It could be a challenging decision. Sometimes it's a crucial conversation I'm worried may go badly. Often, it's simply the pace and amount of work coming up that I'm just not sure I have the capacity to do that day!

And then I take some time with God through meditation, scripture reading, prayer, and journaling, and suddenly I'm changed. Rather than feeling overwhelmed and anxious, I feel excited and energized! It's incredible! It really is because of this "source of resiliency!"

I can't imagine my life and my leadership without it!

This isn't meant to put pressure on you to believe what I or others believe. This is simply naming a piece of the "Grind, Don't Quit" puzzle that has been vital for us and many others. We trust that you will find your own way in your own time ☺

Jim:

From my perspective, I can't imagine starting my day without devotions, prayer, reading, meditation, and journalling. This is sacrificed time for me that transforms me into my best self for the day. I gain clarity on what to push on, what to back off on. Somedays I get unexpected ideas, and somedays I get clarity that a direction I was thinking of taking isn't the right one. Some days I get the answer, but some days I don't. I just know that this time is critical for me to be prepared for the day.

There was a time in my life when I would be on email as soon as I got out of bed, or have a quick shower and then head to the office or go to a breakfast meeting. Since starting this morning ritual over six years ago, I can count on one hand the number of breakfast meetings I've attended, and the number of times I didn't at least do some type of morning ritual before heading out. At a recent conference Jamie and I attended, it was said, "As leaders we ask ourselves what we need to do, but before we ask that question, we need to ask what I need to do to take care of myself." This is a great question to ask, and by taking care of yourself, you can build up your resiliency.

WAYS TO LIVE THIS OUT

Here are some ideas that might help you execute this chapter and all that has been described. Maybe these are things you used to do. Or maybe you're already doing them. Or perhaps one of these might be something you begin and then experience the power of stepping into a source of resiliency beyond your own efforts and means.

1. Talk to someone you know who seems to have this one nailed. You know they're a person of faith. Take some time to have a coffee and ask them about it. What difference does it make to their life and leadership? What do they do daily to live into this?

2. Consider having an "anchor verse" of scripture that guides you and acts as a mantra you can come back to every day, or in those moments when you struggle, wrestle, and wonder if you can keep going. It might be one of the verses mentioned in this chapter. It might be a favourite quote. Here are some options. Feel free to choose one of these ☺

> **Joshua 1:9** *Have I not commanded you? Be strong and courageous. Do not be afraid; do not be discouraged, for the Lord your God will be with you wherever you go."*

> **Philippians 4:6** *Do not worry about anything, but in everything by prayer and supplication with thanksgiving let your requests be made known to God. And the peace of God, which surpasses all understanding, will guard your hearts and your minds in Christ Jesus.*

> **1 Peter 5:7** *Cast all your anxiety on him because he cares for you.*

> **2 Timothy 1:7** *For God did not give us a spirit of timidity, but a spirit of power, of love and of self-discipline.*

> **Isaiah 40:29** *He gives power to the weak and strength to the powerless.*

> **Philippians 4:13** *I can do all this through him who gives me strength.*

3. Consider developing a morning ritual. There's something about being intentional with the way you start your day. Our research and observations show that many of the most successful people have a morning ritual that sets them up for success for the day. And in most of these examples, there's an element of a Higher Power or leaning into their faith in a God who walks with them through the day. It can be as simple as starting each day by drinking a glass of water and feeling the new life of God flowing into you. It can be taking five minutes to step outside and breathe in the fresh air, feeling the warmth of the sun on your face as you surrender this

day to God. It can be reading a passage of scripture and reflecting on it for fifteen minutes. It doesn't need to be long, but it can change the way you enter the day!

We hope this chapter encouraged you. Part of the reality of leaning into a source of resiliency beyond yourself is that you don't have to go it alone. You have a resource to tap into that can help you keep going, be more creative, and find a power greater than anything you could imagine. You are loved, adored, and of immense value, simply because you're you! And *that* may be all you need to know to keep going and to "grind, don't quit!"

A PERSONAL STORY—STEVE ALLIN

The workplace can often present significant challenges. At one point in my career, I reported to a new senior leader and found that we had completely different ways of working and communicating. Over a significant period, despite much conversation with my new boss and attempts to find a way forward, it became clear to me that I needed to find a new job. It was a decision I came to somewhat reluctantly. I loved the job. I had found the work both challenging and fulfilling, and I loved the team that I led. I was proud of the work we did and how we did it, and I had plans for further advancement. However, the stress of the working relationship, and the impacts it had on my team as well as on me and my family, was taking a significant toll.

Throughout this period, I had been intentional about discerning how to proceed. Working on a difficult relationship is tough and stressful, and changing jobs and employers is fraught with risks: income, job satisfaction, and more. In my faith journey, I had come to know that God was the source of goodness in my life, and that I could put my trust in Him. My discernment process included prayer—seeking God's guidance—as well as many conversations with my wife and those closest to me and regular journaling.

While the job change felt forced on me, it seemed that it could be an opportunity to consider what was next for my life. Through my discernment, I discovered that I wanted to move forward being consistent with the values I held and to follow a path where I could best use my skills and passions to make a difference in the lives of others.

I have not looked back but continue to seek God's guidance in my life.

A PRAYER OF ENCOURAGEMENT

Loving God, you are the ultimate source of resiliency.
We pray for everyone reading this prayer to come to know that you can provide all they need to get through whatever they are facing.
May they know that you are walking with them every step of the way.
May your confidence, your peace, and your love provide them with the energy, wisdom, and power to keep moving forward.
Amen

CHAPTER FOUR:

Mind the Gain, Not the Gap!

INTRODUCTION

If you've ever been to London, England and on "the tube" (subway), you're familiar with the recording that comes on when people are moving in and out of the cars: "Mind the gap!" This recording can become monotonous if you're paying attention, and it also can become a bit of a joke for tourists, because you can find yourself say "mind the gap" in almost any situation. That may be just my sense of humour. I'm not sure the effect it has on the locals. I assume it's just noise, and their subconscious is triggered to mind the gap when moving in and out of the car—or they just don't pay attention to this important safety message.

Our spin on "mind the gap" is a little different. Yes, you must measure and track the distance you still must travel to accomplish your goal, but it's just as import to reflect on your gains as you move toward your goal. This is where you'll get power and build momentum.

In December 2020, I encountered a significant health crisis, which resulted in complete liver failure, a ten-day stay in hospital, followed by over two months of recovery. It was a near-death experience, as for the first eight days in the hospital, I just kept getting worse, with no obvious explanation. Finally, on the eighth day, the amazing team of doctors and pathologists at Oakville Trafalgar hospital started to narrow down the problem, and on day ten they concluded that I'd had an allergic reaction to an antibiotic in late November. There were some dark days in the hospital, but once I got home and gained a little strength,

I decided to go outside and walk. Well, it was more like a Tim Conway shuffle. (For those of you who are too young to know who Tim Conway is, you should check it out on YouTube.)

The goal was to walk around the double block of where we live within thirty days. I was weak and still recovering from liver failure and all the complications that come with it, but I just wanted to return to normal life. I wanted to exercise. I wanted to be outside! I never thought when I set the goal to improve my health by eating better and exercising daily that I would miss exercising, but I did.

So I set out on day one and walked to the corner; on day two I walked to the first driveway, and on day three I walked to the third driveway. Each day I went just a little further. You get the picture. The goal was to walk around the block, but every day I measured the gain by driveways. That's how I reached my goal—measuring the gain, not the gap, one shuffle at a time. To be clear, before I set out on these shuffles, I had a nap, and when I got back, I had a nap, but it was looking at how far I'd come, not how far I had to go, that made it possible.

Measuring the gain and not the gap moved me forward when, frankly, it would have been easier to quit. By the week of January 18, I'd reached my goal, so I changed the goal in terms of distance and regularity.

On these walks, I was accompanied by people who encouraged me and cheered me on, which made each step easier. I'm sure that some friends thought they might have to carry me home, but I appreciate and love each one of them. Their support and encouragement meant so much to me. There will be more on support and accountability partners in Chapter Five, including how they help to make the journey to the goal more endurable, rewarding, and fun.

GETTING REAL

So how do you get started?

The first step is to decide how you're going to measure achievement by breaking it down into bite-size bits that you can track and measure. A couple of old sayings really ring true on this: "Inspect what you expect" and "You can't improve what you don't measure." Measuring is fundamental to goal achievement.

However, this can be hard, because you have a gap between where you are and where you want to go. It can initially be exciting to see the vision, and you start to move toward it, but things get in the way and obstacles appear, which can lead to discouragement. This is when you must know what you're measuring, keep measuring, and take time to look back to see the progress you're making and celebrate it! Maybe it's a private celebration, or maybe you tell a family member or friend. Measuring the gain fuels your motivation to keep going.

There's a concept in measuring progress called "lead measures" and "lag measures." In *The Four Disciplines of Execution*, the authors do a terrific job of explaining these terms in detail, but what follows is the explanation in a nutshell.

A lag measure tells you how you are tracking toward a goal. It measures the outcome. For weight loss, you'll get on the scales and weigh yourself. It's done after the fact, after the eating, exercise, and sleeping that help you lose the weight.

In business, it's your financial statement that shows the financial picture for the previous month, quarter, or year. It shows your results, whether your goal has been achieved or not.

In running, it may be the time it takes you to run the 5k distance. It tells you the outcome. Lag measuring plays a key role in measuring progress after the performance. It can be rewarding if you're moving toward your goal, but it can be discouraging if you're not. In our experience, if you're only using lag measurements to track progress, it can end with abandonment of the goal, frustration, and disappointment.

When you use lead measures in combination with lag measures, however, the magic starts to happen. A lead measure is an action that, if done consistently, will produce the outcome you desire and move the lag measure in the direction of your goal. With a lead measure, you have full agency over whether you take the action or steps that will lead to the desired outcome. The tracking of lead measures can be fun and rewarding but also provide feedback if you're going off track.[1]

Here are some of our examples of how we have used lead and lag measurements.

Jamie has a goal for attendance at Alpha. Measuring the attendance after the fact is a lag measure. So what is the lead measure? He knows that despite all the advertising and marketing that leads up to an Alpha, the best way to get people to attend is through personal invitation, and they can be especially impactful if they come from him. Therefore, the lead measure is tracking the number of

---

1 Chris McChesney, Sean Covey, and Jim Huling, *The 4 Disciplines of Execution* (Salt Lake City, UT: FranklinCovey Co., 2012), 45.

personal invites for the four weeks leading to a new Alpha, which coincides with the other communications.

Jim has a sales target for his business, so the financial statements show how he is doing. That's the lag measure. So what is the lead measure? A considerable number of their sales are quoted prior to them getting the contract, so they measure the dollars quoted each week, which accumulates into each month, then each quarter. This is the lead measure. If they don't have enough quotes, they won't have enough sales. However, when you dig a little deeper, you need to understand how we quote the opportunities, which is by calling on prospective clients. So another lead measure is if we're making enough sales calls to support the quote targets. We have agency over that.

We used the same system in drafting this book. Jamie had experience with writing a couple of books previously, but I have never authored a book before, so we had to figure out a way to get the book done. Our lead measure became spending thirty minutes writing every other day, because we knew if we put in the time, the words would get written. By tracking this lead measure, we knew if we missed Monday, we had to schedule it for Tuesday, and so on. These blocks of times became focused deep work time with no interruptions.

When it comes to measuring, celebrating the gains and not being focused on the gap is the big idea. You have more agency than you may think to act!

A goal can become overwhelming if you keep looking at the gap. Looking at the gain can fuel your motivation and give you confidence that you're moving in the right direction. It's easy to get discouraged and disappointed and then not take the necessary action. You might even abandon the goal before you've really given it your best effort.

When you're grinding toward a goal, you need to find ways to be empowered, and measuring the gain and not the gap is your secret weapon. Why is this the case? Because you can act on the lead measure. You are in control.

There will be times when you can't, and that's ok. Have grace with yourself and decide when you'll be able to act. Maybe you have a health issue or a busy season in your career, or the children need some extra attention. We all have things that come up, but once that season is over, you can get back in the game and start again, if the goal is still something you want to achieve.

You can say yes to the necessary time to put in the effort, and say no to the distraction. In every no there is a yes. In saying no to the distraction, you're saying yes to your goal, yourself, and your vision for your life.

CELEBRATING!

Celebrating can be hard for goal-setters and achievers because there's always another mountain to climb, but we've found this to be a major way to gain further fuel for moving toward achieving the goal. In a lot of ways, we gamify it for the smaller wins, and we celebrate the bigger wins in bigger ways. A lot depends on you, but we'd encourage you to find ways to celebrate.

We often use the power of timing deep work, so we turn off all distractions and hunker down for thirty, sixty, or ninety minutes. But once that timer goes off, we reward ourselves, or celebrate, by having a snack, or we'll send an encouraging text to each other, go for a quick walk around the block, or sit and have a coffee with someone. This allows us to get a sense of reward and accomplishment, and it fuels us for the next action we need to take.

For bigger milestones, we might go for dinner or do something special. Since we really started living into this idea of celebration, we've had more champagne than ever before. Just the act of opening the bottle with family and friends and going around lifting a glass and stating what or who you're grateful for is an act of celebration that will fuel you for the next time you need to act and grind. Celebrate along the way and don't just wait for the big reward or celebration once the goal is achieved. There can be as much pleasure in the journey as in the actual achievement of the goal.

We'd like to share a story of celebration from 2019. Our friend Steve Allin is the Executive Director of The Journey Neighbourhood Centre, a non-profit organization that serves a marginalized neighbourhood in our city. One of their major fundraising events takes place in the fall and is called Ride for Refuge. In 2019, Steve took it on to lead the entire ride. He had goals for the number of participants, for the dollars to be raised, and for the number of volunteers. He and his team worked hard to make this happen. It was a beautiful autumn day and a tremendous success.

That night, Steve and his wife, Mary Ann, Jamie and Katrina, and Sherry and I all got together to celebrate the day, including the results and the impact it would have in the neighbourhood. We also celebrated the support Mary Ann gave Steve through the planning and execution of the event. But most importantly, we wanted to celebrate Steve and his determination to put this event on, and his grind, don't quit attitude in the process. We had a bottle of champagne and some food, and we stood around the counter and went around and around until the champagne was done celebrating! It was great! As goal-setters and achievers, we're sad to admit that this doesn't always happen, but we try to do it regularly and ultimately give thanks for all God is enabling us to do.

WAYS TO LIVE IT OUT:

1. Brainstorm ideas for lead and lag measures for the goal you want to achieve. Be creative and ask for help from others who may have achieved what you're trying to accomplish, or just someone who you know will support you in reaching your goal.

2. Build a score board so you can measure. Make it easy, visible, and colourful.

3. Track your progress! Daily is ideal, as you want to keep the momentum. This allows you to decide to take the necessary action today if you missed yesterday. If you're competitive, gamify this tracking to give you the energy you need to keep going.

4. Set celebration milestones! Involving others can be a fantastic way to add to the celebration, but small, private celebrations can be fun, as long as you get the sense of celebration and treating yourself!

5. Have grace with yourself when you miss and be sure to enjoy the journey even when it's hard, because the best part of achieving a goal is the journey.

A PERSONAL STORY—SIMON WILCE

I have the privilege of running a nonprofit called Christians Against Poverty. We help families in financial crisis, with a core mission value being to spread "across the nation"—not so we can have a big organization, but because we want to impact as many lives as possible. We began in the United Kingdom twenty-seven years ago and have gone a long way to achieving that aim. I also had the privilege of pioneering this in New Zealand and seeing it spread across the nation there since it launched in 2008.

When I moved to the United States in March 2019 with the same goal, I knew the gap between starting and covering a nation was our biggest ever! This is a nation of 331 million people, thirty-seven times bigger than New Zealand and with a land mass forty times bigger than the United Kingdom! Yet I had high expectations of fast growth. Fast forward four years, and with the impact of COVID, we haven't yet achieved half of what I had dreamed of compared to other launches. The gap remains huge.

That's why I'm so encouraged by the concept of "mind the gain." If I just switch my perspective, I look out at a network of over thirty centres, over $1 million dollars raised in that time, and having already helped hundreds of low-income families with their finances—all things other organizations may dream of achieving!

I remain ambitious for more impact, but minding the gain keeps me focused on the blessings I have seen and the good we have done.

PRAYER OF ENCOURAGEMENT

Dear God,
Sometimes we're so hard on ourselves.
As I strive to move forward in my life and in my leadership,
Help me to see the progress that has already happened
And not get so fixed on how far I still want or need to go!
Increase my awareness of the blessings I have already experienced,
And may that give me confidence that you will give me all I need
To continue to move forward.
Amen!

CHAPTER FIVE:

The Power of an Accountability Partner

INTRODUCTION

This may be the single biggest idea of this book as we outline how our partnership developed and the ways our lives and leadership grew as a result. We will also give some ideas on how it can work for you.

Jim:

I started this journey in the fall of 2016 by attending a live event called Free to Focus in Nashville, hosted by Michael Hyatt. The content moved me to see a vision for my life and business like I'd never had before. I was getting reenergized but knew I had a long way to go. In the fall of 2017, I asked Jamie to come along to Nashville for a two-day Free to Focus intensive. He agreed to come, with some hesitation, because he felt he already had a great system, but he committed to joining me on the trip. It was amazing, and it was the start of a life-changing experience for both of us.

A few weeks after returning from Nashville, in a Starbucks in Mississauga between his son's basketball games, I presented Jamie with a proposal for a partnership of personal and professional growth. I knew my chance of achieving my goals was much greater by doing it with someone, and I couldn't think of a better person to do it with. After some prayer, thought, and discussions with Katrina, Jamie agreed to join me on the journey that has transformed our lives and leadership!

We believe that the following scripture summarizes the fundamental idea of what has happened as we've journeyed together, and it has become our anchoring scripture for what we do:

> Two are better than one,
> because they have a good return for their labor:
> If either of them falls down,
> one can help the other up.
> But pity anyone who falls
> and has no one to help them up.
> Also, if two lie down together, they will keep warm.
> But how can one keep warm alone?
> Though one may be overpowered,
> two can defend themselves.
> A cord of three strands is not quickly broken.
> Ecclesiastes 4:9–12

We know that we have been blessed with a special partnership because we support, encourage, and hold each other accountable in all areas of life and leadership. It may not be possible for you to have just one person, but we encourage you to try to find someone. If not, look for a partner who can support you in each of your goals. This is a two-sided coin, however, as you must commit to supporting them as they reach for their goals.

Jamie:

I would echo the significance of an accountability partner. It has been amazing to see the power and strength this brings to your life. You really do feel like you're not alone, and when it comes to some of the hard things we need to do, that is so important! There are days when I know Jim is cheering me on and praying for me. There are days when I feel like Jim's accomplishments are my accomplishments. It makes celebrating better and the challenges easier.

A specific example of this took place when I was trying to introduce quarterly meetings into our organization. This wasn't something we had done before at the church. In some ways, it was changing the culture, and that's never easy! However, it was also a meaningful change for me, and I was dragging my feet on it. Seeing Jim lead these meetings with his company, and seeing the impact it made, motivated me to move past the internal barriers and make it happen. Jim's encouragement and excitement, which came through regular texts of support, were helpful for me to keep at it, especially when things were hard, busy, or I didn't want to do it. Most people don't want more meetings, or struggle with these kinds of changes, until they see how effective and necessary they are. Now we're at a point where our team looks forward to these quarterly gatherings as we envision the future, deepen our connections as a team, and lead more effectively together. It would have been almost impossible for this to happen without the support of an accountability partner.

GETTING REAL

So how does it work?

STEP 1: BE VULNERABLE

It can be hard to be open, honest, and vulnerable with someone, but that's where it starts.

You need to share your vision for your life and your desires and goals to achieve that vision. Be open about why you want to achieve it, what you think the first few steps to achievement will be, and the timeline you want to work toward.

Now comes the demanding work: you need to share your fears about trying to work toward your vision. This is the limiting belief that you feel is holding you back and the new, liberating truth that you're adopting.[2]

A limiting belief is a thought or some sinking thinking that limits your potential and sets up a boundary in your mind that convinces you that you can't achieve the goal you desire. Limiting beliefs for me centred on my health: "I have never exercised regularly and never will," "I don't have the discipline or strength to exercise," "I have never been fit, and I never will be." And these are just a few!

Think of a limiting belief as a rope tied around the ankle of a baby elephant, with the other end tied to a big spike. This restricts the elephant from moving beyond the length of the rope, creating a limiting belief in the elephant. He starts to believe that if a rope is tied around his ankle, he can't go any further than the length of the rope. As the elephant grows, this mindset remains, to the point

2 Michael Hyatt, *Your Best Year Ever* (Ada, MI: Baker Books, 2018).

that even though his size would easily allow for the spike to be pulled out of the ground, the elephant won't even try. You may have seen this at a circus and wondered why the elephant didn't keep walking. It's because he doesn't think he can.

A liberating truth is the opposite of a limiting belief. It's a truth about the situation that allows you to change your mindset to increase your belief that you can achieve your goal.

We all have ropes around our ankles that we've come to believe limit our abilities, but in many cases it's just not true. There may be truth in some beliefs—for example, as a fifty-eight-year-old man, standing at five-foot-ten, I can't become an NBA player. However, I can learn some skills to play some basketball in a pickup game for fun and exercise. I could change my limiting beliefs on my health and many other things, and so can you.

This is how I changed some of my limiting beliefs to liberating truths with the help of some coaching and encouraging from Jamie:

Changing "I have never exercised regularly" to "I can exercise for thirty minutes today."

Changing "I don't have the discipline or strength to exercise" to "I can get stronger by exercising every day."

Changing "I have never been fit, and I never will be" to "I'm getting healthier every day."

This can be hard, as you will be sharing deeply. We want to assure you, though, that it's worth it. The more honest and open you are with your support partner, the more they can help, support, encourage, and give you the odd kick in the butt.

It's hard to be this open because we all have ego and pride at some level, but if you can share, will be deeply rewarding. Always remember that the more you share, the more space and comfort you'll give your support partner to share when it's their turn.

STEP 2: BRAIN TRUST

Now that you've shared with your support partner, you need to begin developing what some have called a brain trust. This is when you really begin to get coordinated and remain connected as you travel the journey.

As a support partner, you can call out or get called out when your partner is slipping into their limiting belief, and you can encourage them with their liberating truths. This is a balance between encouragement, accountability, and providing insights. Let's dig a little deeper on how this works.

Encouragement involves offering inspiration, motivation, and a cheering of the other on. In providing encouragement, you're breathing into the other person the courage to continue the track they're on. We've all been there; we're discouraged, and often that's a result of the limiting beliefs rising in us, creating fear and doubt. Your role as a support partner is to always be encouraging and provide your partner with the courage to continue. To accomplish big goals, there will be setbacks, and it will require courage.

Accountability is a little different from encouragement. It means to hold your support partner to their commitments and goal. Through this process, you want to be kind but not soft. As you follow up with them, ask questions like: Did you do this task? Did you make those calls? Did you connect with that family member? If they say no, then you must ask why. This can be a challenging conversation, and sometimes there are real reasons, but in some cases it will be an excuse. You must keep digging and reminding them of the why behind their goal. It's their goal, and maybe something has changed to make them want to revise their goal, which is fine, but it's your responsibility to help them uncover this.

Our experience has been that sometimes the priorities have changed, but if this isn't clear, inaction can stall other goals, creating self-doubt, raising limiting beliefs, and reducing motivation. In the worst-case scenario, one might abandon all stop moving forward.

Providing insights to your partner can bring clarity and ideas for reaching their goals. Jamie provided insight to me on my fitness journey after several months of just walking and push-ups. He encouraged me to start doing other body weight exercises. He introduced me to Tabata, group 60 Minute HIT training, strength training, and even added in tennis and cycling. I'm sure he has more up his sleeve too!

Jamie's insights have helped me not get bored with my present routine, stretched me physically and emotionally, and led me to a more balanced approach to my fitness and health. I still remember the first time I went to HIT training. I was so out of my comfort zone, so intimidated, but through the encouragement of all who were there, it became a regular activity we did weekly for months.

This is the dance between encouragement, support, and providing insights that comes from a brain trust between accountability partners.

STEP 3: COMMUNICATION RHYTHM

You'll need to find a rhythm for the cadence of support and accountability. This will depend on the type of goal you're sharing and the consistency of the new habit you're trying to implement. It can be a combination of lead or lag measures, but we encourage lead measures, because if we're hitting our lead measures, we have a better chance of achieving the goal.

Here are some ideas:

If it's a health or exercise goal, it could be a daily text to let your partner know you've done the work. The accountability partner needs to reach out if they haven't heard from you by an appropriate time.

If it's a weekly professional goal, it could be handled in a summary email at the end of the week, reporting on the results.

If it's a goal to improve a relationship, maybe it's a text at the beginning of the week letting your accountability partner know that you plan to connect with a certain person. As the week unfolds, you can let them know when you've completed the goal.

We share a photo of our weekly preview from the Full Focus Planner on Monday morning, then we flip each other a quick text of encouragement about one or two items. We also pray for each other and our goals throughout the week.

We encourage you to have a rhythm for meeting face to face. This could be weekly, monthly, or quarterly, depending on the depth and level that you want to share. You might have different partners for different areas of your life, and they may each have their own and specific rhythm.

One of the most important pieces of our personal organization is a quarterly review. We try to book a day to go through the review. We complete our reviews independently and then review our results and goals, milestones, and new habits we want to implement. We also review together our personal and organizational vision narratives and talk about how we're moving toward them. This can be extremely helpful because your partner may see progress that you don't because you're focused on griding it out. Remember, mind the gain, not the gap. The quarterly review is a terrific time to rejoice and reconnect to the goal, revise, remove, or replace it, and then reset accountability and support check points.

There will be bumps along the way to achievement, which is why this support partner plays such a vital role

There were days in my health journey when, frankly, I didn't want to do my exercise, but I felt I couldn't let Jamie, as he had invested so much in helping, encouraging, and training me. So those days I did it for Jamie! My pride and ego wouldn't let me quit. Some days I did it so I could send the text to Jamie to say it was done, and on some days, I could brag about a new personal best or surprise him with an activity he didn't expect. I have learned that the sending and receiving of texts created a dopamine hit in my brain. Dopamine is a happy chemical that you get during the anticipation of doing an activity. It's addictive, and you begin to crave it. It can also be generated by other activities, such as posting and getting likes on social media streams. This along with the endorphins being ignited during the exercise moved me to a place where I became addicted to exercise.

This is the power of an accountability partner. They can support, encourage, remind you of your why, and hold you accountable until you see the results of the new habits and goal achievement. With years of goal setting, this has become the secret ingredient to achievement that we never experienced before.

As we've worked together in this support and accountability role, we've also grown in our lives and leadership in many ways. We're more focused, more present in the moment, enjoying what life has to offer in many more ways. It's been a blessing to us, our families, and the organizations we lead. We truly are living into the principles that our future is bigger than our past and that the best is yet to come.

It's available for you. All you need to do is invite someone into your life. You may need a couple of people who can support you in the different goals you want to achieve, but it starts with an invitation. We believe that people want to help other people, so invite them into your life. Hey, maybe they'll say yes and invite you into their life.

It's a fantastic way to live and a terrific way to grow and move toward your ideal life.

Yes, you will have to be vulnerable, and it can be scary, but it's worth it!

Yes, it takes work, determination, and effort, but your goals are worth striving for!

WAYS TO LIVE THIS OUT

The first step for you may simply be to make a list of potential accountability partners. Have some fun listing names of people you may want to reach out to or be more connected with.

Perhaps you want to have several accountability partners for different areas of your life. Again, list some of those areas and match that area up with a person you could both help *and* who could help you in that area of your life.

Maybe you already have accountability partners, and you may want to reach out and thank them or tell them the impact they're having in your life.

Ok, now it's time to take this beyond an idea. Right now, text or call someone you think would join you on a journey of growing together in your life and leadership, and ask them to give you thirty minutes to share an idea with them. We hope that they'll say yes and that your journey together will start. We believe in you and in the future you want to achieve for yourself.

A PERSONAL STORY—LEXI BLACK

Having accountability partners has made a dramatic difference in my life. I've been attending Jim and Jamie's quarterly Growing Together in Life and Leadership sessions for the past three years. As a direct result of these sessions, I started to focus on areas of my life that needed work—my health, my finances, my professional life, and my relationships. I created a three-year vision script and identified annual goals to work toward. All of this was a huge leap from the person I used to be, but I'm convinced I wouldn't have been as successful at achieving my goals, or even articulating them, without the support of key individuals.

At the Growing Together sessions, I connected with two other women in church leadership roles, and we decided to meet regularly to check in with each other, share our vision script and goals, and support each other during the day-to-day challenges at work and in our lives. This was during a time of isolation during COVID, and these weekly check-ins were helped to keep me motivated and feel less alone. While our life situations have changed over the years, I continue to meet with one of the group members on a bi-weekly basis, checking in on how we're doing, sharing our successes and challenges, and supporting each other.

I also have a close friend who has become my accountability partner, especially as I work toward my health and financial goals. She's my running partner, and often we talk about how we're doing as we run in the early hours of the morning. We've shared our annual goals and encouraged each other as we work toward them. She's someone I trust and can be vulnerable with, who I know will support me and hold me accountable.

We've also embarked on common goals together, such as hiking the Bruce Trail end to end and signing up for a triathlon. There's no way I would have found the courage to sign up, train for, and participate in a triathlon without having a partner to encourage me along the way! Our goals aren't always the same, but we check in with each other and support each other. And we celebrate achievements! My accountability partner knows how hard I've been working toward my goals, so when I make progress in an area, she celebrates with me, understanding the magnitude of the achievement. She also helps me keep things in perspective, challenges me on some of my assumptions, and keeps me grounded. Just as putting my goals down on paper makes me that much more likely to succeed, sharing them with someone I trust who supports me along the way makes them that much more real and attainable.

A PRAYER OF ENCOURAGEMENT

Dear God,
Thank you that you made us to be in relationship with others,
And that we really can be better together than we can be on our own.
I appreciate the people in my life who already help me keep going,
Not quit or give up, and strive to be the best I can be.
Help me be open to connecting with others in ways that we can grow together.
Amen.

CHAPTER SIX:

The Secret of Small Actions

INTRODUCTION

Have you heard the best way to eat an elephant? They say "one bite at a time!"

Isn't that so true?

When we have something before us that just seems too big to tackle, and we aren't sure how or even *if* we're going to get it done, the best way to move forward is simply one step at a time!

This is the secret of small actions. We don't need to have the whole project figured out. We don't need to have all the money in hand. We don't need to have everyone on board. We don't need to know the whole picture. We don't have to completely see the end of the road. All we need to do is to know what the next step is and courageously take it and see what comes next.

Sometimes it's as simple as doing research, sending one text, sharing an idea with someone else, or creating a document or even that old school type of checklist to guide us toward next steps. When we do this, it opens up a whole new world!

This simple little secret can move us from despair to hope, from paralysis to empowerment, from being stuck to opening new possibilities. It can change our perspective and help us believe that the impossible *is* possible—by simply taking one little action and moving the needle just a little bit!

As we think about taking small actions to accomplish massive things, I'm reminded of those amazing stone walls in England. I always marvel when we drive around the countryside there and see these waist-high stone walls running for miles and miles! I can't help but think to myself, *How in the world did someone build this?* One time when travelling with a relative from England, I asked that question, and the answer was so simple and so true! They said, "It's pretty simple ... one stone at a time!"

Someone, or many people, took the time to find one stone and place it on the wall. And they did that over and over and over again!

Perhaps on a day when they felt like the task was too much, or that it was going to be impossible to build this wall *that* far, they held on to this one idea. Maybe at a moment when they wondered if there were enough stones in all the world, let alone their little corner of the planet, to build a wall like this, they had to remind themselves of this little secret: Just keep going! Put *one more* stone on the wall! That's all it is! Imagine that a stone wall miles and miles long that caused people to marvel for centuries came about because some people had the discipline to put one stone on at a time and create something beautiful and amazing!

We can do amazing things that seem impossible if we can get our heads around the idea of this chapter. It's the secret of small actions, small actions that over time can lead to incredible things.

GETTING REAL

You may like this concept very much. It makes sense, and you agree with it in theory. But perhaps you're wondering how to apply it. What does this even look like?

Let's drill down a bit here!

First, START EASY

Sometimes simply recognizing an easy step you can take today will help move things along. When we're paralyzed by the magnitude of a project or goal, sometimes it's good to do something we know we can do. It can give us confidence and may even help us get excited again rather than simply living in the land of "this is just too big!" For example, for the longest time I wanted to start a podcast, but I have no idea what went into doing a podcast. I'm not the most technically savvy person in the world, so this whole project, as much as I wanted to do it, was overwhelming for me.

So what's an easy step or task I could do to move this one along?

I could call someone who's already doing a podcast and ask about how they started and what they do to "make a podcast happen." There's an even *easier* step than that! Having the conversation is really a second action. The first action is to set up a meeting to discuss their podcast via an email, text, or direct message. It might take five minutes if I take time to craft what I want to say, but at the most, that's *five minutes*! Five minutes to take an action that starts to advance something I was almost paralyzed around.

That is the secret of simply starting with small actions.

A SECOND idea is CREATE A LIST OF SMALL ACTIONS.

Sometimes we just don't know what to do. We haven't taken the time to brainstorm what we need to do to make this happen. We do this in many areas of our lives.

When we go on a trip, we often make a list of the things we need to pack. When we head to the grocery store, we make a list of what we want to purchase. When we get up on a Saturday morning, we might create a list of tasks we want to do that day. These lists empower us and give us direction. We have clarity, purpose, and a sense of what needs to happen to be "successful."

As we face the challenges of life or look at things we want to do that might be overwhelming, creating a list can help us move from being stuck to even getting excited about the possibilities.

Let's say you have an idea about something you want to do that has been in your head for some time, but you've been struggling with moving it forward and are getting frustrated. In fact, when you even think about it, you immediately want to stop thinking about it because it scares or overwhelms you. (That may be happening right now! Sorry about that!) But here's the thing: If you take a few minutes to list some possible actions to move this project forward, you might get the breakthrough you've been looking for. This list will become your plan, and you'll have a sense of what needs to happen next. You will see the path forward.

Here's an example from my life and leadership. I've had an idea for some time for our church, but I haven't moved it forward yet. It's pretty simple, and I think it could have a significant impact. The big idea is to create a system that allows us to remember and celebrate milestones and life events in our congregation, such as weddings and the loss of loved ones for whom we've done funerals. Wouldn't it be awesome to send notes of encouragement and congratulations to couples on their first, fifth, twenty-fifth, and even fiftieth anniversary!

A crucial element in all of this is to remember *why* you want to do this in the first place. Without this, we can find ourselves lacking the motivation to take one of these actions or steps, even if they're easy to do. Remembering our *why* will help us get to a place where we want to move forward.

As you think about something that's been hard to accomplish, write down *why* it's important to you. If you want to become healthier but have struggled with that, *why* do you want to be healthier? Maybe you want to live a long life and be active with your grandchildren. Maybe you have great purpose in your life and want to be able to keep working and leading with maximum energy. You might just want to finally get at this because you've been talking about it for years, so it's a matter of personal integrity!

As you get clear on your reasons, your motivation will increase. Making that phone call, asking someone to join you in this task, or even doing research all require energy and motivation. Remembering your why will help with that, and you may find yourself not only doing one action but taking several steps toward your goal. This kind of momentum can help you move this forward!

This certainly worked for me, as I was struggling with even getting started writing this book. I just wasn't motivated and couldn't bring myself to take the time to start writing. This continued to be a challenge for several months! I would *want* to start writing but just couldn't get myself to take the time to do it!

As I reminded myself of *why* this was important, I started to *want* to get going on it. For me, this book was important to do for several reasons. Many of us struggle to keep going, and I wanted to get this book done to help people "grind, don't quit." Also, I was looking forward to doing this with my friend Jim Christian, as this was something we'd talked about for several years. I have a long-term goal of writing twenty books with twenty different people, and the clock is ticking, if you know what I mean! All these reminders of *why* this was important helped me get motivated and start writing!

WAYS TO LIVE THIS OUT

Getting started is more than half the battle! Once you get started by taking just a simple action or two, it's amazing how things start to unfold. You'll also have momentum on your side! Just like a little snowball rolling down a hill collecting more snow and getting bigger and faster, you'll find that same power as you take some action and small steps toward your goal.

Here are some practical ideas that might help you get started:

1. Share your idea or project with someone. It's amazing how this helps with accountability. If chosen wisely, that person may even end up helping you accomplish what you want to do. Minimally, you will have gained confidence and conviction as you share this and have someone cheering you on, encouraging you, and even challenging you to get at it.

2. Get something into your calendar. What gets scheduled gets done. Nothing ensures that you'll do something as much as putting a day and time to it. It's as simple as taking the first ten minutes of the day to work on this project, or scheduling your walk at noon every day for twenty minutes. You simply schedule that you're going to make a phone call to get this initiative started next Wednesday at 3:00 p.m. As simple as this is, it helps you not only remember to do something but to be accountable to yourself.

3. Consider taking Psalm 119:105 as your mantra and motivation. This beautiful scripture verse simply says, "Thy Word is a lamp unto my feet, and a light unto my path." The meaning is so powerful. In the day when this was written, a lamp was simply a candle in a holder that would light up the path just enough to take the next step. However, once you took that step, you could then see *just* far enough to take the *next* step. And so on. As you trust God enough to take that next step, even when you can't see beyond it, you have found your way down the path. This is a helpful principle and mindset when committing ourselves to small actions that can lead us to our goals.

4. Ask for help. Sometimes we don't even know the right actions or steps to take. Don't be afraid to reach out and talk to someone who has done this before. They will be honoured that you asked and excited to share what they've learned and how they've moved forward. If you're having trouble losing weight or getting to where you want to be, reach out and have a coffee with someone who has recently done that. If you want to

author a book or start a podcast, have a chat with someone who has done that already. If you're leading a project but aren't sure how to go about it, check in with someone who has been there and done that!

Hopefully this chapter has helped you consider the power of small actions and the secret of taking one more step, as small as that might be, toward bigger goals and visions. You've heard it said that "Rome wasn't built in a day." This is a fantastic way to summarize what we're trying to say here. It means that it takes time to build or create remarkable things, and doing things slowly over time can be transformational.

I have not yet been to Rome, but everyone I know who has gone has come back telling me how incredible it is! They describe in detail the beauty and majestic nature of a city with a great history. When it comes to those things you want to accomplish that may seem outside your current abilities and bandwidth, please keep Rome in mind. Someone had a vision that took time to complete. It really wasn't built in a day. But that doesn't mean it wasn't possible or that what you desire to accomplish isn't possible either!

You don't need to have the whole thing figured out to start.

All you need is ...

One step at a time.

One action after another.

That's all it's going to take.

You can do this!

A PERSONAL STORY—DR MARISSA CANNING AND DR ANDREW CHELLADURAI

Marissa and Andrew graduated from a naturopath medicine program and decided to start their own practice together. This venture would require great resiliency and a "grind, don't quit" spirit!

Starting your own business is one of the most challenging things anyone can do. For Marissa and Andrew, there were times when they wondered if they were going to make it! There was blood, sweat, and sometimes even tears!

As they reflect over the first two years of practice, they realize it was those small actions that really helped them get to where they are today. Little things like a morning ritual to keep them healthy and strong. Little things like having a vision for their lives and practice. Little things like taking time for a date night and enjoying time together. Little things like getting a website together. Little things like honouring every single patient so that they would refer their friends and family to the practice. Little things like praying together to tap into a source greater than themselves and find that flicker of hope when things were tough. All these small actions add up to a growing business, where they now have a two-week waiting list! Amazing!

Just like Andrew and Marissa, you too can practise the secret of small actions to progress and accomplish your dreams!

PRAYER OF ENCOURAGEMENT

Gracious God,
Thank you for being with us in the small actions that can move us forward,
Especially when we find ourselves tired and challenged to keep going.
May you bring resiliency to continue,
Wisdom to find the right next steps,
And the courage to put one foot in front of the other.
Give us hope that as that happens,
We will get to where you are leading!
Amen.

CHAPTER SEVEN:

The Leadership Challenge

INTRODUCTION

It's one thing to make the intentional decision ourselves to "grind, don't quit." It takes everything we have and more to not give up, to keep going despite all the challenges, to get up each day and take one more step, even though we don't feel like it!

It takes everything we have to do that some days.

I get it. I've been there. It is hard. So hard!

And that makes *this* chapter an even greater challenge, because the "greatest challenge" is not just to make this kind of decision ourselves. An even greater challenge is helping others make this same intentional decision to keep going and not give up in adversity!

How do we lead others into this mentality and mindset? How do we help our teams to keep going and give it one more try each day? What can we do to manage morale, offer encouragement, and enable those we work with to join us in this journey of "grind, don't quit"?

In this chapter we'll explore this crucial element of our leadership role. Don't worry if you're asking yourself some big questions, such as "How can I help others do this when I'm not even sure I can do this myself?" Others have led the way, and as we explore how they've done this, we'll glean wisdom and ideas that will help us get a better handle on this part of our leadership. For some of us, it may simply be the awareness that this is part of our job and that we really can empower others to make these same kinds of decisions.

This may be the greatest challenge, but it's also the greatest opportunity. We can build into other people's lives and make a difference. We can help people we care about reach another gear in life and leadership.

Here's a story that shows us what that can look like, and even more importantly, what that can feel like! Over the years I've been blessed with some amazing leaders, and I am grateful for all of them! One of the best was a basketball coach I had in high school. His name was Mr. Cutler. He was tall and intense. He *loved* the game and *loved* his players and *loved* to help people get better at both the game of basketball and at life!

When he walked into the gym, you just wanted to play hard. You wanted to get better and execute some of the things he had taught you. You knew he'd be watching with the expectation that this was what you would be doing.

There was something about him. Here are a few things I remember as being significant to how he did this:

- He clearly modeled this for himself. He was a life-long learner. He was getting better every day. He watched videos, followed other coaches, and brought all of that to our team. There was no question that he was continuing to grow and get better himself!

- There was no question that he was the leader of the team. It wasn't that he didn't ask others to be part of things. We had a manager and assistant coaches, and he certainly invited us as players to lead at different times. But at the end of the day, it was clear that he knew it was his responsibility to know the temperature of the room and to make sure we were moving in the right direction.

- He made this expectation part of our team's culture. You knew the day you made his team that you'd be required to work hard and "grind, don't quit." There were no other options. This was what we would do because this was who we were!

- He made things fun as well. I don't want to paint a picture of a tyrant here. This was someone who loved life and loved us, and although it came with some lofty expectations and intensity, there was never any question that he loved us all and would do anything for us. He often went out of his way to make it fun and ensure everyone was having a good time!

You may have someone in mind from your life who was a leader who helped you grow and do things that you may not have been able to do on your own. What was it about them that you remember? How did they encourage you through times of challenge?

One last memory of Mr. Cutler was how he lived through this challenge of helping others rise to the occasion. We were in the finals of a huge tournament, and a time-out was called with just seconds on the clock. As we huddled on the bench, Mr. Cutler gave some final instructions as we prepared to go out and finish the game. I don't remember what he said, the score, or who won the game! What I do remember is what he did just before we went back on the court. As we started to get up to walk onto the court, he realized that we were all completely nervous and there was an anxiousness in the air—which is very normal at that moment! He called us back for just a moment and said, "Guys keep this in perspective! There are billions of people around the world who don't give a &*%^$#* about what happens in this game!"

We all laughed, relaxed, went out, and played the last few seconds of the game. And we went differently because of what he said and did!

We have that same opportunity and ability as we recognize the greatest challenge of enabling others to also "grind, don't quit."

GETTING REAL

One of the ways I love to think about this challenge is that I'm helping people see that they have another gear. So often we're limited by what we *think* we can do or what we've done in the past. We might also be limited by the people around us who carry these limiting factors and share them with us too often. Sometimes we wonder if we have the energy, creativity, or time to take things to the next level.

Well, when you realize you have another gear, a whole new world opens! One of the most important roles of a leader is to help people see that, know that, believe that, and live into that!

Here are three things that might help us take on this assignment that we call the greatest challenge: helping others to keep going and "grind, don't quit."

1. Recognize that this is our job!

   Many times, I have spoken with leaders who talked about their team or their organization as if they personally weren't a part of it. It can be very subtle, but the red flags go up for me when I start to hear people say "they." "They" just aren't into it. "They" aren't working hard enough. "They" don't get it. "They" just don't have it in them.

   This may sound a little harsh (but don't forget this chapter is called "The Greatest Challenge" ☺), but it's *our* job to help people grow, rise to the challenge, and reach another gear that can take them and us to the next level. If we really want to be this kind of leader, the first step is to recognize that this is part of our job! In fact, it may be one of the most important parts of our job!

2. Be honest and real.

   Sometimes we can get frustrated with those people who are so positive that they miss the reality of the current circumstances. Again, this book is about who we're trying to be when things get hard. And step one is naming this openly and with full disclosure.

   People need to know that we know. They need to trust that we also recognize that this might be one of the most challenging times we've ever faced. We're not meeting the budget right now, and if things continue, we'll be out of business in six months. Morale is at an all-time low, and we all feel it. There's a sense of division in our team and organization that's preventing us from fulfilling our mission and work. These things need to be said and named.

   Our role starts with naming this for people. As we do, people will be relieved that we know this too, because chances are they already know this! People will reach another level of trust as we offer transparency and authenticity. We can even express our concerns and feelings.

All of this is part of living into the greatest challenge. However, what comes next is equally important, because we don't want to leave people there!

3. Offer hope and a plan.

As leaders, if we only left things at the "reality check," we'd be leaving people without hope. That wouldn't be good. That would be unfair! Proverbs 29:18 says *"Where there is no vision, the people perish"* (KJV).

Once we outline the reality of the situation, we'll want to be clear on what we can do to work through this, build some momentum, and be part of the solution. We want to share the vision of a better future and what it's going to take to get there.

My experience has been that no matter how hard things are, people *love* to see a plan and are inspired to know that we *can* do something about this! You may not even know if it will work yet, but that's ok. You can even say that. It's ok to be honest and transparent. However, it's not ok as a leader to *not* have a plan of action and to leave people paralyzed in the pain of analysis and your current reality.

You might catch yourself trying to us phrases like the following:

"Yes, it's hard, but let's do it anyway!"

"If it were easy, everyone would be doing it!"

"Let's try this and see what happens!"

"It may not work, but at least we're trying, and if this doesn't work, it may lead us to what will!"

It's all about keeping a balance between the reality of the challenge and the hope that we can work toward something new. As we do that, we enable others who we are leading to keep going, especially when it's hard.

WAYS TO LIVE THIS OUT

Often we wonder what we can do to encourage and challenge others to rise to a new level. As a leader, that's one of the most important things we can do. Here are a few ways that we hope will help you with that.

1. Write out what you want to communicate to people. Often these issues are extremely sensitive, so you need to be careful how you communicate. Put something in writing that names the challenge and what can be done about it as an organization or leadership team. This will help you to be clear with yourself and also bring clarity for others.

2. Look at diverse ways of communicating this message. It may be a video sent out to the team, or an email. Work it into all of your one-on-one meetings. Name it in every staff meeting for as long as you need to. Get creative. People will appreciate your work on this, and because of the time you've taken to share the message, they'll know how important this one is.

3. You may have heard the idea that "vision leaks." It's true. This means that even when you're sick and tired of saying this same message, and you think you've already said it too many times, you need to keep communicating it, especially if it's a challenging time and message.

4. Look for others to also help you communicate this message to the team. There are people on every team who can influence others. Sometimes they can have an even greater impact on certain people. These people will be honoured that you've invited them to help lead at this level.

This chapter is titled "The Leaders' Greatest Challenge" for a reason! It's hard. It's complex. It's scary. It's all of this and more. However, it's also an opportunity.

My experience has been that those things that are the most challenging are often ones that God blesses the most. And that certainly is true here. We have the chance to make a difference exponentially as we enable others to rise to the challenges of life and leadership. We have the opportunity to leave a legacy that will go way beyond the current challenges. This is legacy-making stuff here!

The people we lead will look back and remember that they were led by someone who refused to give up. Years from now, they'll remember that they were enabled and encouraged to keep going and not give up despite the odds. They will translate this "grind, don't quit" mentality into other areas of their lives. They'll tell their grandchildren about this chapter of their lives when they had this incredible leader who just refused to let the circumstances get the best of them, and as a result, they accomplished what seemed at the time to be impossible!

And guess what—that leader can be you!

That leader is you!!

As you do this, you will have turned the greatest challenge into the greatest opportunity. And the people you lead will be forever grateful!

A PERSONAL STORY—BRAMPTON FIRE CHIEF BILL BOYES

Bill Boyes is the Fire Chief for Brampton Fire & Emergency Services, so he knows all about leading others. Bill does an amazing job of keeping himself motivated and moving forward. Part of his responsibility is to lead others to do the same.

As the entire world experienced, COVID brought with it incredibly complex and challenging situations for leaders. Through the pandemic, Bill was faced with unbelievably tough decisions that needed to be made quickly and would impact many people, including his firefighters, as well as our whole city of Brampton. The realities of change and the need for constant adjustments were unprecedented.

Bill was able to not only survive but to thrive and lead well through these times because he is both humble and confident. He has the humility to ask others their opinions and listen authentically, combined with the confidence to act, decide, and then adapt as needed.

The challenge of leading through tough times is possible for Bill because he leans on his team and others who are part of his life. This network of relationships is a key ingredient to life but also to leadership, especially when we're empowering others to keep going through tough times!

A PRAYER OF ENCOURAGEMENT

Loving God,
On those days when I can barely get going myself,
I pray for your strength and wisdom to lead others.
It might be my team at work, or my family at home.
Give me the energy and compassion and inspiration
To share with these people I love so much
And want to help move forward in what we're called to do together.
Amen.

CHAPTER EIGHT:

When to *Not* Grind

INTRODUCTION

This may seem like a strange chapter in a book about resiliency, working hard, and fighting through the tough times to keep going, keep pushing, keep driving, keep running, keep on keeping on despite all the odds! Yet this may be the chapter that resonates with you the most!

Sometimes we need to stop pushing and *not* "grind, don't quit." Sometimes the best thing we can do is press pause for a while. Sometimes we need to rest, catch our breath, wait, and just be ok with that. There's a flip side to being all about pushing and driving all the time—sometimes we can push too hard!

I will never forget the conversation I had with my wife, Katrina, one Friday night. It was more a conversation that *she* had with *me*! We were sitting by the fire enjoying a glass of wine together and reflecting on the past week. I was in a season where I used the word "intentional" *all the time*! I desired to be more intentional in all aspects of my life: our marriage and how we were growing together, my leadership at the church, the goals I was setting, our parenting, our finances, and my health and working out. Getting tired yet? I am even just writing this!

Katrina turned to me and said, "You know what—you're always talking about being intentional these days. I wish you could sometime be less intentional!"

Whoa! That got my attention!

We had an honest conversation about what was going on, and I discovered that night—and repeatedly since then—that sometimes I need to slow down, rest, relax, and *not* push. It may be for a season, a day, or an hour, but there is power in pausing, which is just as important as knowing when and how to push forward.

That is what this chapter is about. And it may be the most important thing you take away from this book.

GETTING REAL

As we think about recognizing when it's time *not* to grind, or to take a pause rather than keep pushing, we may think of times when we've done that. Many years ago, I was preparing for my very first sermon. I was quite anxious about it, to be honest. It was a new thing for me, and I hadn't even been to seminary yet, so I'd taken no classes on how to do this. It was a deep dive into something I had never done before.

I remember being quite excited at first. I was sitting at the computer and flying along, preparing a manuscript, and then about halfway through I got stuck! I didn't know where to go or how to finish the message. The more I struggled, the more I wondered if what I'd already put down was any good either! Self-doubt, confusion, and uncertainty started to fill my mind, and it was all downhill from there into a sea of frustration. I had no idea what to do!

So I called a mentor and they gave me some advice that would guide me for the rest of my life. They told me to "walk away." Take a break. Press the pause button.

And that's what I did ...

I came back to it later, and everything had changed. I loved what I'd written so far, and I had clarity and excitement about how to finish the message. I was back in the game!

Sometimes we just need to walk away.

When the wallpaper isn't going on the way we want, or the parts aren't fitting together for that new BBQ, or that song or poem just isn't coming together, we need to give ourselves a little break and sometimes *stop* pushing.

Take a breath.

Relax for a moment.

Leave some space for grace.

And then, and sometimes only then, we will find ourselves ready to keep pushing, driving, and moving forward again—but in a new and better way!

A PERSONAL STORY—TED BROWN, CEO REGENERATION OUTREACH

Ted is a great leader and realized he was being called to take a break and not push harder. Through his reading of scripture and time of prayer, this need to press pause became increasingly clear. Ted was also experiencing the reality of increased workload due to COVID and the extra demands and complexities that were very real for him.

As a result, Ted finally took a sabbatical after thinking and talking about it for two to three years. Three massive things were part of the growth that took place during this time away.

1. Renewal of the importance of his relationship with God as Ted was filled up and energized rather than feeling depleted.

2. Recognizing the importance of family as they were able to spend extra time together.

3. The opening of new creativity as he stepped back from the day to day and had time for other things, like woodworking.

Regeneration not only survived while Ted was off, but there were opportunities for others to step up in new ways. Ted came back with greater focus and drive than ever before.

A PRAYER OF ENCOURAGEMENT

Dear God,
As much as I'm wired to push, strive for more, and work hard,
Sometimes it's best just to rest and take a break.
Help me know when to hold off
And take a breath, trusting that you are at work beyond me.
Keep me open to your grace
And bless me and others with the wisdom
To know that you are there
In the resting and waiting
As much as you are in the working!
Amen.

CHAPTER NINE:

We Almost Didn't Write This Book

INTRODUCTION

Something crazy happened in the writing of this book.

It was called COVID.

You may have heard of it. Maybe it impacted your life too!

Both of us found our worlds and organizations tuned upside down. We lost staff, and our team changed overnight. It took a full year to recover, as we both were required to step in and take on roles we hadn't done for quite some time. We needed to fill in gaps and help new people transition into new roles and do extra work just to survive.

We agreed that this little *Grind, Don't Quit* project needed to be put on hold. But once we stopped, it was hard to start back up again. To be honest, it was more than hard. We found ourselves stalling, procrastinating, and getting exceptionally good at naming reasons why we just weren't able to get at finishing this book.

And then one day we realized how sad it would be to *not* finish a book with the title *Grind, Don't Quit*!

GETTING REAL

The bulk of the writing took place in the summer of 2021, as we had developed a rhythm that allowed us to work on it on a regular and consistent basis. But as the fall of 2021 rolled around, and another wave of lockdowns set in, some key changes in our organizations took place, and we need to stop writing just short of the finish line.

Then as 2022 rolled around, my wife, Sherry's, health deteriorated, and she was fighting for her life. Other things were going on as well, and the limiting belief was rising that this story wasn't worth telling. Who would want to read about me? Jamie? Yes, for sure, but not about me.

Thanks to the principles outlined in this book, it is finished. At various times we had to apply these principles, so we decided when not to grind in the fall of 2022. We had to mind the gain, not the gap in December 2022. We remembered our why of wanting to write a book that someone might read one day when they were about to quit. Hopefully this book would give them the energy and power to keep going. And we had an accountability partner to push each other forward. Better together moved us to finishing the book.

Perhaps you can relate to this reality. Perhaps you have started a project or initiative that you almost didn't complete when it got hard.

COVID and this global pandemic might have had huge implications for your life too and led to some changes that you're still trying to catch up from. And maybe because of that, it's time to reach another gear.

Jamie:
Our son Caleb is playing high school basketball, and I love going to watch. I'm a huge fan of sports, and I like it even more when one of our kids are playing! One of the reasons I *love* watching this basketball team is because they never give up! They have a resiliency that is greater than almost any team I've ever seen. They're not the best basketball players; in fact, most of them haven't even played before. They are extremely good athletes, and they work hard every minute they're on the court!

But what really sets them aside is that even when they could be down, they just keep going and never stop fighting. They may miss some layups, have some bad turnovers, and make some mental mistakes—which can be frustrating to watch at times! But I have never seen them give up! They just keep coming, battling, and working hard, and it works!

They may not win every game, but they always have a sense of accomplishment because they don't stop trying!

WAYS TO LIVE THIS OUT

1. Acknowledge We Are Tired

We may need to acknowledge that COVID has had an impact on us. We may feel the need to rest or make some changes before we give it our all again.

2. Remember our WHY

Several times in this book we've been reminded to remember our why. That's ok, because sometimes we need to come back to that, especially when we reach the wall or go through something as impactful and all-consuming as COVID.

Make a list of WHY we want to author that book, or work out every morning, or eat differently, or make that call, or save that money, or whatever it is we're struggling to get to or finish.

3. Talk to Someone

One of the ways we realized how sad it would be to not finish this book was when we shared that with someone, and they laughed at how ironic that would be! Their response was helpful in naming the reality that we really did want and needed to finish this!

Jim found this little poem that seemed like the perfect way to end this chapter:

> "When things go wrong as they sometimes will,
> When the road you're trudging seems all up hill,
> When the funds are low and the debts are high
> And you want to smile, but you have to sigh,
> When care is pressing you down a bit,
> Rest if you must, but don't you quit.
> Life is strange with its twists and turns
> As every one of us sometimes learns
> And many a failure comes about
> When he might have won had he stuck it out;

Don't give up though the pace seems slow—
You may succeed with another blow.
Success is failure turned inside out—
The silver tint of the clouds of doubt,
And you never can tell just how close you are,
It may be near when it seems so far;
So stick to the fight when you're hardest hit—
It's when things seem worst that you must not quit"

– John Greenleaf Whittier

PRAYER OF ENCOURAGEMENT

Loving God,
Thank you for all that you do to carry us through the valleys and setbacks of life.
And all that you do give us the power to keep going.
Thank you that you are the same God of the mountain tops as the valleys of life.
You are so faithful.
We pray for each person reading this prayer, that they know you are with them every step of the way.
And that will be more than enough
To keep going
And to "grind, don't quit!"
Thank you, Lord,
Amen.

Bibliography

Hyatt, Michael. *Your Best Year Ever*. Ada, MI: Baker Books, 2018.

McChesney, Chris, Sean Covey, and Jim Huling. *The 4 Disciplines of Execution*. Salt Lake City, UT: FranklinCovey Co., 2012, 45.

Printed in Canada